THE ROYAL HORTICULTURAL SO

WILD IN THE GARDEN

DIARY 2019

The Royal Horticultural Society
Wild in the Garden Diary 2019
© 2018 Quarto Publishing plc

Photographs © individual photographers as listed in Picture Credits
Text copyright © the Royal Horticultural Society and printed under licence granted by the Royal Horticultural Society, Registered Charity number 222879/SC038262.

For more information visit our website or call 0845 130 4646. An interest in gardening is all you need to enjoy being a member of the RHS.
Website: rhs.org.uk

Astronomical information © Crown Copyright. Reproduced by permission of the Controller of Her Majesty's Stationery Office and the UK Hydrographic Office (www.ukho.gov.uk)

First published in 2018 by Frances Lincoln an imprint of The Quarto Group,
The Old Brewery, 6 Blundell Street,
London N7 9BH, United Kingdom
www.QuartoKnows.com

A catalogue record for this book is available from the British Library

ISBN: 978-0-7112-3950-0

Printed in China

9 8 7 6 5 4 3 2 1

Front cover Goldfinch (*Carduelis carduelis*) on a teasel
Back cover Wood mouse (*Apodemus sylvaticus*) on a blossom-laden branch
Title page Great tit (*Parus major*) and blue tit (*Cyanistes caeruleus*)
Introduction Honey bee (*Apis mellifera*)

RHS FLOWER SHOWS 2019

The Royal Horticultural Society holds a number of prestigious flower shows throughout the year. Details can be found by visiting www.rhs.org.uk or telephoning the 24-hour Flower Show Information Line (020 7649 1885).

PICTURE CREDITS

All photographs are from Shutterstock ©
Martin Pateman Front cover; **davemhuntphotography** Back cover; **Martin Fowler** Title page, Week 31, Week 42; **rockyclub-r007** Introduction; **Ondrej Prosicky** Week 2; **Erni** Week 3, Week 29, Week 39, Week 46, Week 50, Week 52; **Hannu Alicja Korbinska** Week 4; **Hannu Rama** Week 5; **Morgan Stephenson** Week 7; **Angyalosi Beata** Week 8; **MAC1** Week 9; **Mirko Graul** Week 11; **Florian Andronache** Week 12; **Ian Sherriffs** Week 13; **Bernd Wolter** Week 14; **Robert Adamec** Week 16; **BHJ** Week 17; **Soohyun Kim** Week 19; **KOO** Week 20; **Stefan Rotter** Week 21; **Maciej Olszewski** Week 22; **Jolanda Aalbers** Week 24; **Chrislofotos** Week 25; **Sally Clarke** Week 26; **Rasmus Holmboe Dahl** Week 28; **hjochen** Week 30; **Sari ONeal** Week 33; **Anton Dumitrescu** Week 34; **Christopher P. McLeod** Week 35; **bartrak** Week 37; **J. Need** Week 38; **Jiri Hera** Week 41; **L. Galbraith** Week 43; **Targn Pleiades** Week 44; **John Navajo** Week 47; **Abi Warner** Week 48; **Paul Rookes** Week 51; **Artush** Week 1

MIX
Paper from responsible sources
FSC® C008047

CALENDAR 2019

JANUARY
M	T	W	T	F	S	S
	1	2	3	4	5	6
7	8	9	10	11	12	13
14	15	16	17	18	19	20
21	22	23	24	25	26	27
28	29	30	31			

FEBRUARY
M	T	W	T	F	S	S
				1	2	3
4	5	6	7	8	9	10
11	12	13	14	15	16	17
18	19	20	21	22	23	24
25	26	27	28			

MARCH
M	T	W	T	F	S	S
				1	2	3
4	5	6	7	8	9	10
11	12	13	14	15	16	17
18	19	20	21	22	23	24
25	26	27	28	29	30	31

APRIL
M	T	W	T	F	S	S
1	2	3	4	5	6	7
8	9	10	11	12	13	14
15	16	17	18	19	20	21
22	23	24	25	26	27	28
29	30					

MAY
M	T	W	T	F	S	S
	1	2	3	4	5	
6	7	8	9	10	11	12
13	14	15	16	17	18	19
20	21	22	23	24	25	26
27	28	29	30	31		

JUNE
M	T	W	T	F	S	S
					1	2
3	4	5	6	7	8	9
10	11	12	13	14	15	16
17	18	19	20	21	22	23
24	25	26	27	28	29	30

JULY
M	T	W	T	F	S	S
1	2	3	4	5	6	7
8	9	10	11	12	13	14
15	16	17	18	19	20	21
22	23	24	25	26	27	28
29	30	31				

AUGUST
M	T	W	T	F	S	S
			1	2	3	4
5	6	7	8	9	10	11
12	13	14	15	16	17	18
19	20	21	22	23	24	25
26	27	28	29	30	31	

SEPTEMBER
M	T	W	T	F	S	S
						1
2	3	4	5	6	7	8
9	10	11	12	13	14	15
16	17	18	19	20	21	22
23	24	25	26	27	28	29
30						

OCTOBER
M	T	W	T	F	S	S
1	2	3	4	5	6	
7	8	9	10	11	12	13
14	15	16	17	18	19	20
21	22	23	24	25	26	27
28	29	30	31			

NOVEMBER
M	T	W	T	F	S	S
			1	2	3	
4	5	6	7	8	9	10
11	12	13	14	15	16	17
18	19	20	21	22	23	24
25	26	27	28	29	30	

DECEMBER
M	T	W	T	F	S	S
						1
2	3	4	5	6	7	8
9	10	11	12	13	14	15
16	17	18	19	20	21	22
23	24	25	26	27	28	29
30	31					

CALENDAR 2020

JANUARY
M	T	W	T	F	S	S
	1	2	3	4	5	
6	7	8	9	10	11	12
13	14	15	16	17	18	19
20	21	22	23	24	25	26
27	28	29	30	31		

FEBRUARY
M	T	W	T	F	S	S
					1	2
3	4	5	6	7	8	9
10	11	12	13	14	15	16
17	18	19	20	21	22	23
24	25	26	27	28	29	

MARCH
M	T	W	T	F	S	S
						1
2	3	4	5	6	7	8
9	10	11	12	13	14	15
16	17	18	19	20	21	22
23	24	25	26	27	28	29
30	31					

APRIL
M	T	W	T	F	S	S
	1	2	3	4	5	
6	7	8	9	10	11	12
13	14	15	16	17	18	19
20	21	22	23	24	25	26
27	28	29	30			

MAY
M	T	W	T	F	S	S
				1	2	3
4	5	6	7	8	9	10
11	12	13	14	15	16	17
18	19	20	21	22	23	24
25	26	27	28	29	30	31

JUNE
M	T	W	T	F	S	S
1	2	3	4	5	6	7
8	9	10	11	12	13	14
15	16	17	18	19	20	21
22	23	24	25	26	27	28
29	30					

JULY
M	T	W	T	F	S	S
		1	2	3	4	5
6	7	8	9	10	11	12
13	14	15	16	17	18	19
20	21	22	23	24	25	26
27	28	29	30	31		

AUGUST
M	T	W	T	F	S	S
					1	2
3	4	5	6	7	8	9
10	11	12	13	14	15	16
17	18	19	20	21	22	23
24	25	26	27	28	29	30
31						

SEPTEMBER
M	T	W	T	F	S	S
	1	2	3	4	5	6
7	8	9	10	11	12	13
14	15	16	17	18	19	20
21	22	23	24	25	26	27
28	29	30				

OCTOBER
M	T	W	T	F	S	S
			1	2	3	4
5	6	7	8	9	10	11
12	13	14	15	16	17	18
19	20	21	22	23	24	25
26	27	28	29	30	31	

NOVEMBER
M	T	W	T	F	S	S
						1
2	3	4	5	6	7	8
9	10	11	12	13	14	15
16	17	18	19	20	21	22
23	24	25	26	27	28	29
30						

DECEMBER
M	T	W	T	F	S	S
	1	2	3	4	5	6
7	8	9	10	11	12	13
14	15	16	17	18	19	20
21	22	23	24	25	26	27
28	29	30	31			

GARDENS AND WILDLIFE

Gardens as a network form an important ecosystem. An ecosystem is an interdependent and dynamic system of living organisms which is considered together with the physical and geographical environment. They are interdependent because everything in a garden depends on everything else.

The garden ecosystem is extremely variable thereby offering year-round interest. Gardens offer a large number of animals the perfect conditions for different stages of their life cycle. Insects may prefer sunny, sheltered spots to forage and mate, but their larvae may need to live in water or in rotting vegetation. The large range of garden wildlife is there because of gardening not despite it.

Due to the nature of gardens, groups of species that exploit a network of gardens' resources find abundance over a longer time period, compared to what a single natural site can offer. Even gardens that are managed without regard for wildlife still offer some benefit, especially when they are considered as part of the total garden network. Even without simulated 'wild' habitats, gardens are living, diverse ecosystems in their own right. No garden is too small to provide some benefit to wildlife. Many visiting animals can actually be residents of neighbouring gardens. It is the garden network that is of overall importance to wildlife, forming the larger garden ecosystem.

City gardens are important corridors facilitating the safe movement of birds, butterflies and other wildlife. Wildlife friendly gardens don't need to be messy, with an abundance of stinging nettles. All gardens offer some resource to certain species, however, with a little thought and planning, every garden can be of great benefit to a much wider range of species. Look around your local area and see what type of habitat is missing and whether it is possible for you to provide it: perhaps a pond, nest-boxes, decaying wood, or an undisturbed leaf pile? The more diverse habitats provided, the greater the varieties of birds and wildlife visiting your garden.

The RHS recognises and actively promotes the valuable contribution that gardens make to wildlife, believing that with thoughtful management it is possible to enhance the wildlife potential in any garden without compromising the gardener's enjoyment of it. For more information visit: **www.rhs.org.uk** and **www.wildaboutgardens.org.uk**

'Leave food out in case hedgehogs emerge for a quick food foray before returning to hibernation'

JOBS FOR THE MONTH

- Hang bird feeders and put out food on the ground and bird table.
- Make sure the bird bath is topped up and the water is not frozen.
- Regularly clean the bird bath and table.
- Make sure the pond does not freeze over.
- Leave out food for hedgehogs (*see* Week 36).

BEES

Encourage bees into the garden:
- Provide them with flowers from February to November.
- Plan your planting to include clumps of bee-friendly plants in sunny places.
- Allow daisies and dandelions into your lawn.
- Avoid double or multi-petaled cultivars of plants.
- Avoid all pesticides.
- Create nest sites for solitary bees in sunny spots such as hollow stems (bamboo canes or herbaceous plant stems), cardboard tubes can be purchased and holes (2–8mm) can be drilled into fence posts.

BIRDS

Blackbirds, thrushes, tits and robins will be visiting the garden.

Food: Birds appreciate a helping hand at this time of year as many natural sources of seeds and berries will now be exhausted. As well as bird seed, mealworms and fat balls can be purchased from specialist suppliers and will provide much-needed fat and protein. Don't rush to clear windfalls and rotten fruit from the ground as these provide food for blackbirds, thrushes and fieldfares. Make your feeding regime as consistent as possible to encourage birds to return regularly.

Water: Regardless of the weather, a regular source of unfrozen water is essential for drinking and bathing so keep containers topped up and ice free. Change bird bath water regularly and periodically scrub out bird baths using specialist detergent (available from bird food suppliers). Always wear suitable protective clothing kept especially for these tasks.

DECEMBER & JANUARY 2019

New Year's Eve

Monday **31**

New Year's Day
Holiday, UK, Republic of Ireland, USA, Canada,
Australia and New Zealand

Tuesday **1**

Holiday, Scotland and New Zealand

Wednesday **2**

Thursday **3**

Friday **4**

Saturday **5**

New moon
Epiphany

Sunday **6**

JANUARY

7 *Monday*

8 *Tuesday*

9 *Wednesday*

10 *Thursday*

11 *Friday*

12 *Saturday*

13 *Sunday*

Tree sparrow (*Passer montanus*)

JANUARY

First quarter   *Monday* 14

Tuesday 15

Wednesday 16

Thursday 17

Friday 18

Saturday 19

Sunday 20

Great spotted woodpecker (*Dendrocopos major*)

JANUARY

21 *Monday*

Full Moon
Holiday, USA (Martin Luther King Jnr Day)

22 *Tuesday*

23 *Wednesday*

24 *Thursday*

25 *Friday*

26 *Saturday*

Australia Day

27 *Sunday*

Last quarter

Grey squirrel (*Sciurus carolinensis*)

JANUARY & FEBRUARY

Holiday, Australia (Australia Day)

Monday 28

Tuesday 29

Wednesday 30

Thursday 31

Friday 1

Saturday 2

Sunday 3

Greenfinch (*Carduelis chloris*)

FEBRUARY

4 *Monday*   *New moon*

5 *Tuesday*   Chinese New Year

6 *Wednesday*   Accession of Queen Elizabeth II
Holiday, New Zealand (Waitangi Day)

7 *Thursday*

8 *Friday*

9 *Saturday*

10 *Sunday*

'Consider building a bee home for solitary mason bees to colonise in the spring.'

PONDS

The fastest way to encourage wildlife into your garden is to build a pond. Within a short period of time a pond will attract birds, amphibians, insects, mammals and a whole range of mini-beasts. Alternatively even a small water feature or a bird bath will encourage wildlife to visit.

Building a pond

- If you build your pond in January/February the first toads may arrive in the spring.
- Choose a sunny site.
- Connect your water butt so it can fill the pond automatically during heavy rain.
- Ensure at least one side is sloping to provide easy access in and out of the water.
- Make sure there is sufficient space around the edge for dense waterside planting as this can provide a safe 'corridor' to hibernation areas.
- Avoid using cobbles and paving around the edges as these surfaces heat up fast in the sun and can be lethal for young amphibians crossing to reach shady areas.
- Create a nearby log pile using the biggest logs you can find. All kinds of insects will love it too.

JOBS FOR THE MONTH

- Put up nesting boxes for birds.
- Keep bird feeders topped up and put food out on the ground and bird table. Avoid foods that could cause choking in young fledglings.
- Keep the bird bath topped up and unfrozen for part of the day if possible. Regardless of the cold, many birds still like to bathe.
- Regularly clean the bird bath and table; dispose of old food.
- Make sure the bird bath and table is kept clear from snow.
- Put out hedgehog food (*see* Week 36).
- Keep the pond from freezing over.

PREDATORS

Protect birds from predators by siting any bird tables and feeders away from areas easily accessible by cats. Remember cats can easily approach via roofs or trees. Placing feeders next to prickly bushes can be a deterrent. You can give birds warning of a potential predator by attaching multiple bells to your cat's collar.

FEBRUARY

Monday **11**

First quarter

Tuesday **12**

Wednesday **13**

Valentine's Day

Thursday **14**

Friday **15**

Saturday **16**

Sunday **17**

Crested tit (*Lophopanes cristatus*)

FEBRUARY

---

18 *Monday*   Holiday, USA (Presidents' Day)

---

19 *Tuesday*   *Full moon*

---

20 *Wednesday*

---

21 *Thursday*

---

22 *Friday*

---

23 *Saturday*

---

24 *Sunday*

Hazel dormouse (*Muscardinus avellanarius*)

FEBRUARY & MARCH

Monday **25**

Last quarter

Tuesday **26**

Wednesday **27**

Thursday **28**

St. David's Day

Friday **1**

Saturday **2**

Sunday **3**

Nuthatch (*Sitta europaea*)

MARCH

4 *Monday*

5 *Tuesday*   Shrove Tuesday

6 *Wednesday*   *New moon*
Ash Wednesday

7 *Thursday*

8 *Friday*

9 *Saturday*

10 *Sunday*

'Create shallow areas in your pond with flat stones to encourage frog spawn.'

JOBS FOR THE MONTH

- Put up nesting boxes for birds.
- Top up bird feeders and put food out on the ground and bird table.
- Avoid chunky foods, such as peanuts, that might cause young fledglings to choke.
- Keep the bird bath topped up and clean it regularly.
- Put out hedgehog food (*see* Week 36).
- Make your pond more wildlife friendly (*see* Week 6).
- Sow or plant a wildflower meadow.
- Hang a bat nesting box.
- Create log and twig piles from prunings and felled trees. This will provide protection and debris for nests.
- Remove any netting placed over the pond to protect it from autumn leaf fall.

MAMMALS & AMPHIBIANS

Look for amphibian spawn in ponds. Frog spawn is usually in jelly-like clumps; toad spawn is in long double strands; newt spawn is laid individually on pondweed stems.

BIRD FOOD & FEEDERS

- Use wire mesh feeders for peanuts (but avoid putting out until fledglings are old enough not to choke).
- Goldfinches love the tiny niger seed which needs a specially-designed feeder.
- Encourage ground-feeding birds such as robins and dunnocks by placing food on wire mesh positioned just off the ground.
- Place fat blocks in wire cages – plastic nets can be dangerous for some birds.
- Create your own fat blocks by melting suet into moulds such as coconut shells or logs with holes drilled into them.
- Clean feeders regularly and move them around the garden to avoid fouling the ground underneath.
- Water containers should be shallow, preferably with sloping sides and no more than 5cm (2in) deep.
- Put out different types of bird food to attract specific species (*see* Week 18).

MARCH

Commonwealth Day

Monday **11**

Tuesday **12**

Wednesday **13**

First quarter

Thursday **14**

Friday **15**

Saturday **16**

St Patrick's Day
Holiday Republic of Ireland

Sunday **17**

European hedgehog (*Erinaceus europaeus*)

MARCH

18 *Monday*   Holiday, Northern Ireland (St. Patrick's Day)

19 *Tuesday*

20 *Wednesday*   Vernal Equinox (Spring begins)

21 *Thursday*   *Full moon*

22 *Friday*

23 *Saturday*

24 *Sunday*

Baby tawny owl (*Strix aluco*)

MARCH

Monday 25

Tuesday 26

Wednesday 27

Last quarter   *Thursday* 28

Friday 29

Saturday 30

Mothering Sunday, UK and Republic of Ireland   *Sunday* 31
British Summer Time begins

Blue tit (*Cyanistes caerules*) fledgling

APRIL

1 *Monday*

2 *Tuesday*

3 *Wednesday*

4 *Thursday*

5 *Friday*   *New moon*

6 *Saturday*

7 *Sunday*

Herald moth caterpillar (*Scoliopteryx libatrix*)

'Keep an eye out for summer visitors such as willow warblers, housemartins, swifts and swallows who will start arriving.'

JOBS FOR THE MONTH

- Put up nesting boxes for birds (see Week 32).
- Top up bird feeders and put food out on the ground and bird table (see Week 18 and Week 23).
- Avoid chunky foods that might cause young fledglings to choke.
- Keep the bird bath topped up.
- Put out hedgehog food (see Week 36).
- Make your pond more wildlife friendly (see Week 6).
- Create log, twig and/or rock piles to provide shelter for wildlife.
- Plant annuals and perennials (single flowers as opposed to double flowers) to encourage beneficial insects into the garden.

BATS

Bats begin roosting now. Bats eat insects including garden pests or nuisance insects like mosquitoes. Bats are a good indication of a healthy, insect-rich environment. There are 17 species of bats in Britain but their numbers have declined. The more common species likely to be seen in the garden are the common pipistrelle, soprano pipistrelle, brown long-eared bat, noctule and Daubenton's bat.

INSECTS

Wildlife encompasses more than birds, bees and butterflies. Every living thing has a role to play in your garden's ecosystem. Many of these 'good' insects are natural predators as well as playing their own role in the food chain.

- Woodlice and earthworms recycle organic matter.
- Ground beetles and centipedes will eat slugs.
- Spiders eat wasps and mosquitos.
- Ladybirds consume huge quantities of aphids as well as other insects and larvae that can damage your plants.
- Lacewing larvae feed on aphids, mites and other small insects.
- Hoverfly larvae are one of the first to become active in the early spring and eat aphids, particularly those in places other beneficial insects can't get to.

APRIL

Monday **8**

Tuesday **9**

Wednesday **10**

Thursday **11**

First quarter

Friday **12**

Saturday **13**

Palm Sunday

Sunday **14**

APRIL

15 *Monday*

16 *Tuesday*

17 *Wednesday*

18 *Thursday*

Maundy Thursday

19 *Friday*

Full moon
Good Friday
Holiday, UK, Canada, Australia and New Zealand

20 *Saturday*

First day of Passover (Pesach)

21 *Sunday*

Easter Sunday
Birthday of Queen Elizabeth II

Wild rabbit (*Oryctolagus cuniculus*)

APRIL

Easter Monday
Holiday, UK (exc. Scotland), Republic of Ireland,
Australia and New Zealand

Monday 22

St. George's Day

Tuesday 23

Wednesday 24

Holiday, Australia and New Zealand (Anzac Day)

Thursday 25

Last quarter

Friday 26

Saturday 27

Sunday 28

Seven-spot ladybird (*Coccinella septempunctata*)

APRIL & MAY

29 *Monday*

30 *Tuesday*

1 *Wednesday*

2 *Thursday*

3 *Friday*

4 *Saturday*   *New moon*

5 *Sunday*

'Look for tadpoles developing their adult "frog-legs". You may see them emerging from the pond and going into the undergrowth.'

JOBS FOR THE MONTH

- Put up nesting boxes (see Week 32).
- Avoid disturbing nesting birds in garden shrubs and hedges.
- Top up bird feeders and put food out on the ground and bird table. Avoid chunky foods that might cause young fledglings to choke (see right).
- Regularly top up and clean out the bird bath and table.
- Make your pond more wildlife friendly (see Week 6).
- Remove weeds from ponds, leaving them on the side for twenty-four hours to allow trapped creatures to return to the water before adding them to the compost heap.
- Create log, twig and/or rock piles to create shelter for wildlife.
- Choose annuals and perennials to attract insects.
- Leave informal hedges un-trimmed for a while to provide food and shelter for wildlife.

MAMMALS

Hedgehog litters are being born and parents may come out to forage at night.

CHOOSING BIRD FOOD

Bird food need not be shop bought or expensive and you can make your own (see Week 10). As well as providing birds with a balanced diet, consider different species' requirements particularly if you want to see more of a particular species in your garden.

Dunnocks crumbs of bread and fat and small seed from the ground

Finches berry cakes

Goldfinches niger seeds

Robins live mealworms

Sparrows, finches and nuthatches sunflower heads

Starlings peanut cakes

Tits insect cakes

Thrushes and blackbirds fruit such as over-ripe apples, raisins and song-bird mix scattered on the ground.

Wrens prefer natural foods but will take fat, bread and seed in harsh winter weather.

MAY

Monday **6**

Early Spring Bank Holiday, UK
Holiday, Republic of Ireland
First day of Ramadân (subject to sighting of the moon)

Tuesday **7**

Wednesday **8**

Thursday **9**

Friday **10**

Saturday **11**

Sunday **12**

First quarter
Mother's Day, USA, Canada, Australia
and New Zealand

Poppies (*Papaver rhoeas*) and cornflowers (*Centaurea cyanus*)

MAY

13 *Monday*

14 *Tuesday*

15 *Wednesday*

16 *Thursday*

17 *Friday*

18 *Saturday*

Full moon

19 *Sunday*

Bank vole (*Myodes glareolus*)

MAY

Holiday, Canada (Victoria Day)   *Monday* **20**

Tuesday **21**

Wednesday **22**

Thursday **23**

Friday **24**

Saturday **25**

Last quarter   *Sunday* **26**

Cabbage white butterfly (*Pieris rapae*)

MAY & JUNE

27 *Monday*   Spring Bank Holiday, UK
                                              Holiday, USA (Memorial Day)

28 *Tuesday*

29 *Wednesday*

30 *Thursday*   Ascension Day

31 *Friday*

1 *Saturday*

2 *Sunday*   Coronation Day

Long-tailed tit (*Aegithalos caudatus*)

'Adult frogs, toads and newts start leaving the pond when the ground is damp.'

JOBS FOR THE MONTH

- Continue to put out food for birds on a regular basis, avoiding chunky foods that might cause young fledglings to choke.
- Consider having a bird bath as it can be a vital source of drinking water for birds. Birds also like to bathe all year. Always clean it regularly and keep it topped up.
- Build a 'ladybird hotel' using bundles of hollow stems or twigs.
- Put up a bat nesting box.
- Put out hedgehog food (see Week 36).
- Thin out, cut back or divide excessive new growth on aquatic plants.
- Create log, twig and/or rock piles to provide shelter for small mammals and insects.
- Use wildlife-friendly slug pellets.
- Mow spring-flowering meadows once bulb foliage has died down.
- Control weeds by mowing recently established perennial meadows.

POND CARE

Aerate the water with a hose and spray attachment. Adding oxygen will aid the fish. Remove dead foliage and blooms.

INSECTS

Hoverflies are in abundance. These harmless insects are good pest controllers, as are wasps. They are also useful pollinators.

MAMMALS

Young mammals are beginning to explore beyond the nest.

PLACING BIRD FOOD

Birds have different feeding requirements (see Week 18) so think about where you are placing food.

Dunnocks ground feeders
Chaffinches bird tables and the ground
Greenfinches anywhere including hanging feeders
Robins bird tables and ground
Sparrows eat anywhere
Thrushes ground feeders but will take from a table
Tits and Nuthatches prefer hanging feeders but also bird tables
Wrens seldom visit feeders or bird tables as they prefer natural food sources.

JUNE

New moon
Holiday, Republic of Ireland
Holiday, New Zealand (The Queen's Birthday)

Monday 3

Tuesday 4

Eid al-Fitr (end of Ramadân)
(subject to sighting of the moon)

Wednesday 5

Thursday 6

Friday 7

The Queen's Official Birthday
(subject to confirmation)

Saturday 8

Whit Sunday
Feast of Weeks (Shavuot)

Sunday 9

JUNE

10 *Monday*

First quarter
Holiday, Australia (The Queen's Official Birthday)

---

11 *Tuesday*

---

12 *Wednesday*

---

13 *Thursday*

---

14 *Friday*

---

15 *Saturday*

---

16 *Sunday*

Trinity Sunday
Father's Day, UK, Republic of Ireland, USA and Canada

Common darter (*Sympetrum striolatum*)

JUNE

Full moon

Monday 17

Tuesday 18

Wednesday 19

Corpus Christi

Thursday 20

Summer Solstice (Summer begins)

Friday 21

Saturday 22

Sunday 23

European peacock butterfly (*Aglais io*)

JUNE

24 *Monday*

25 *Tuesday*   *Last quarter*

26 *Wednesday*

27 *Thursday*

28 *Friday*

29 *Saturday*

30 *Sunday*

Wildflower border on an English allotment.

'This is the season for bat watching.'

JOBS FOR THE MONTH

- Top up bird feeders and put food out on the ground and bird tables (see Week 18 and Week 23).
- Avoid chunky foods that might cause young fledglings to choke.
- Keep the bird bath topped up and clean regularly.
- Plant marigolds around the vegetable patch to attract hoverflies for pest control.
- Put out hedgehog food (see Week 36).
- Construct a hedgehog hibernation box for the coming winter.
- Plant annuals and perennials to attract insects.
- Trim hedges less frequently to allow wildlife to shelter and feed in them.
- Leave nesting birds undisturbed in garden shrubs and trees.
- Avoid deadheading roses that produce hips, as these are a valuable food source.
- Top up ponds and water features if necessary. Aerating the water using a hose with spray attachment adds oxygen, which will help the fish.
- Remove dead foliage and blooms from aquatic plants.

BATS

Bats are excellent pest controllers. All bats are legally protected in Britain and this protection extends to their roosting and hibernation sites. During the day bats hide in dark places like hollow trees so retain old trees with cavities in the trunk where possible. This time of year is the best time to go bat-watching in the evening. Generally they will seek their own spaces but you can provide bat boxes.

- Compost heaps and ponds will generate the type of insects bats like to eat.
- Grow plants with flowers that are likely to attract moths and other night-flying insects. White or pale-coloured flowers are more likely to be seen by nocturnal insects.
- Be insect tolerant. Spare a few caterpillars to feed a bat!
- Avoid using pesticides where possible.

INSECTS

July is flying ant season. Also you will now be seeing an abundance of harmless hoverflies. They are good garden pest catchers. Wasps are also good pest controllers as they eat flies and grubs. They are also useful flower pollinators.

JULY

Holiday, Canada (Canada Day)

Monday 1

New moon

Tuesday 2

Wednesday 3

Holiday, USA (Independence Day)

Thursday 4

Friday 5

Saturday 6

Sunday 7

JULY

8 *Monday*

9 *Tuesday*   *First quarter*

10 *Wednesday*

11 *Thursday*

12 *Friday*   Holiday, Northern Ireland (Battle of the Boyne)

13 *Saturday*

14 *Sunday*

Golden-ringed dragonfly (*Cordulegaster boltoni*)

JULY

St. Swithin's Day

Monday **15**

Full moon

Tuesday **16**

Wednesday **17**

Thursday **18**

Friday **19**

Saturday **20**

Sunday **21**

Common kingfisher (*Alcedo atthis*)

JULY

---

22 *Monday*

---

23 *Tuesday*

---

24 *Wednesday*

---

25 *Thursday*   *Last quarter*

---

26 *Friday*

---

27 *Saturday*

---

28 *Sunday*

Garden spider (*Araneus diadematus*)

JULY & AUGUST

Monday **29**

Tuesday **30**

Wednesday **31**

New moon

Thursday **1**

Friday **2**

Saturday **3**

Sunday **4**

Red squirrel (*Sciurus vulgaris*)

AUGUST

5 *Monday*   Holiday, Scotland and Republic of Ireland

6 *Tuesday*

7 *Wednesday*   *First quarter*

8 *Thursday*

9 *Friday*

10 *Saturday*

11 *Sunday*

'At this time of year many birds enjoy "dust-bathing" as well as splashing about in a bird bath or pond.'

JOBS FOR THE MONTH

- Top up bird feeders and put food out on the ground and bird tables.
- Avoid chunky foods that might cause young fledglings to choke (see Week 18 and Week 23).
- Keep the bird bath topped up.
- Clean bird baths and tables regularly.
- Plant marigolds around the vegetable patch for pest control.
- Put out hedgehog food (see Week 36).
- Make a hedgehog hibernation box.
- Plant annuals and perennials to attract insects.
- Trim hedges less frequently to allow wildlife to shelter and feed in them.
- Leave nesting birds undisturbed in garden shrubs and trees.
- Allow seed heads to develop on some plants as a food source.

HABITATS FOR BIRDS

As natural habitats are destroyed installing or building a nest box is another way to encourage birds to your garden. The main criteria is that they are weatherproof and safe and secure, although certain species favour particular types and locations.

- Wood is the best material but not plywood or chipboard.
- Treat the outside only with a water-based wood preservative (don't use creosote).
- Position away from potential predators and from any feeding area. Angle slightly down to allow water run-off.
- Birds are territorial so avoid multiple boxes in a small area.
- Clean out the box at the end of each breeding season. In October/November scald the inside with boiling water to kill any parasites.
- Leave out over winter to provide shelter in harsh weather.

AUGUST

Monday **12**

Tuesday **13**

Wednesday **14**

Full moon

Thursday **15**

Friday **16**

Saturday **17**

Sunday **18**

Monarch butterfly (*Danaus plexippus*)

AUGUST

19 *Monday*

20 *Tuesday*

21 *Wednesday*

22 *Thursday*

23 *Friday*   *Last quarter*

24 *Saturday*

25 *Sunday*

Honey bee (*Apis mellifera*)

AUGUST & SEPTEMBER

Summer Bank Holiday, UK (exc. Scotland)   *Monday* **26**

Tuesday **27**

Wednesday **28**

Thursday **29**

New moon   *Friday* **30**

Saturday **31**

Islamic New Year   *Sunday* **1**
Father's Day, Australia and New Zealand

Harvest mouse (*Micromys minutus*)

SEPTEMBER

2 *Monday*

3 *Tuesday*

4 *Wednesday*

5 *Thursday*

6 *Friday*

First quarter

7 *Saturday*

8 *Sunday*

'Planting autumn flowering plants will support bees and butterflies.'

JOBS FOR THE MONTH

- Continue to feed birds, avoiding chunky foods that might cause young fledglings to choke (see Week 18 and Week 23).
- Keep the bird bath topped up and clean regularly.
- Construct a hedgehog hibernation box.
- Trim hedges less frequently to create shelter for wildlife. They can also be an important food source.
- Give meadows a final cut before winter.
- Cover the pond surface with netting to stop fallen leaves from entering.

HEDGEHOGS

Hedgehogs are natural pest controllers and eat snails, slugs, beetles, caterpillars and worms. They appreciate supplementary feeding in winter but give them dog or cat food and avoid bread and milk. Hedges offer them some protection when they wander and they like thick dense undergrowth and varying lengths of grass. They hibernate in leaf piles, compost heaps or under hedges or sheds.

BUTTERFLIES

There are 59 butterfly species resident in Britain, plus up to 30 others that are migrant visitors from continental Europe. In the garden you are most likely to see Red Admiral, Peacock, Brimstone, Painted Lady, Comma, Green-veined White, Small Cabbage White and Large Cabbage White. You may sometimes see Orange-tip, Speckled Wood, Meadow Brown, Small Copper and Holly Blue. The Small Tortoiseshell used to be commonly seen but its numbers are in decline.

- Butterflies feed on nectar so plant a range of suitable flowers from March through to October–November.
- In late summer butterflies like Red Admiral and Painted Lady will appreciate fallen fruit left on the ground.
- To support the butterfly you need to look after the young caterpillars so research the plants that will best support them. For example, native ivy supports both caterpillars and adult butterflies.

SEPTEMBER

Monday 9

Tuesday 10

Wednesday 11

Thursday 12

Friday 13

Full moon

Saturday 14

Sunday 15

Fox pup (*Vulpes vulpes*)

SEPTEMBER

16 *Monday*

17 *Tuesday*

18 *Wednesday*

19 *Thursday*

20 *Friday*

21 *Saturday*

22 *Sunday*

Last quarter

Goldfinch (*Carduelis carduelis*)

SEPTEMBER

Autumnal Equinox (Autumn begins)

Monday 23

Tuesday 24

Wednesday 25

Thursday 26

Friday 27

New moon

Saturday 28

Michaelmas Day

Sunday 29

Common frog (*Rana temporaria*)

SEPTEMBER & OCTOBER

30 *Monday*   Jewish New Year (Rosh Hashanah)

1 *Tuesday*

2 *Wednesday*

3 *Thursday*

4 *Friday*

5 *Saturday*   *First quarter*

6 *Sunday*

'Look out for winter migrants starting to arrive from colder, northern regions.'

JOBS FOR THE MONTH

- Top up bird feeders and put food out on the ground and bird tables. All feeds, including peanuts, are safe, as the breeding season is now over.
- Keep the bird bath topped up and clean regularly.
- Put out hedgehog food (see Week 36).
- Construct a hedgehog hibernation box.
- Where possible leave seed heads standing to provide food and shelter for wildlife. If possible leave mature ivy uncut to flower.
- Make a leaf pile for hibernating mammals and overwintering ground-feeding birds; add in some logs to widen the appeal for a greater range of insects; or build a 'bug hotel'.

BIRDS

Look out for redwings, bramblings and fieldfares visiting the garden but don't be surprised if your feeder is untouched. Birds will still be enjoying natural food, which is their preference. However, you can do your bit by making sure your garden offers a natural food 'cafe'.

MAMMALS

Mammals start going into hibernation. If you have a hedgehog hibernating box site it in a quiet shady part of the garden. Leave piles of old leaves undisturbed for small mammals. Take care when turning compost heaps as frogs, toads and small animals may be living there.

INSECTS

Insects need a helping hand to survive the cold weather too. There are some simple things that can be done to help.

- Leaving herbaceous and hollow stemmed plants unpruned until early spring will provide homes for over-wintering insects.
- Plant autumn daisies for butterflies and bees as now there are few other plants in flower for them to feed on. Mature ivy flowers late, providing an excellent nectar source for wildlife.
- Although caterpillars will eat your plants they will grow into butterflies that will help with pollination (and will look beautiful too). Top favourite food for caterpillars includes stinging nettle, thistle, wild carrot, bird's-foot trefoil, buckthorn and blackthorn.

OCTOBER

Monday 7

Tuesday 8

Day of Atonement (Yom Kippur)   *Wednesday* 9

Thursday 10

Friday 11

Saturday 12

Full moon   *Sunday* 13

Blackberries (*Rubus*)

OCTOBER

14 *Monday*

15 *Tuesday*

16 *Wednesday*

17 *Thursday*

18 *Friday*

19 *Saturday*

20 *Sunday*

Elephant hawk moth (*Deilephila elpenor*)

OCTOBER

Last quarter

Monday 21

Tuesday 22

Wednesday 23

Thursday 24

Friday 25

Saturday 26

British Summer Time ends

Sunday 27

Tawny owl (*Strix aluco*)

OCTOBER & NOVEMBER

28 *Monday*

New moon
Holiday, Republic of Ireland
Holiday, New Zealand (Labour Day)

29 *Tuesday*

30 *Wednesday*

31 *Thursday*

Halloween

1 *Friday*

All Saints' Day

2 *Saturday*

3 *Sunday*

Chaffinch (*Fringilla coelebs*)

'Make a simple hedgehog hibernation box to provide winter cover through hibernation.'

IN THE GARDEN

- Always check for hibernating animals before lighting bonfires.
- To melt a hole in ice on a pond, fill a saucepan with hot water and sit it on the ice until a hole has melted. Never crack or hit the ice as the shock waves created can harm wildlife.
- Be careful when turning compost heaps as frogs, toads and small animals often shelter there.
- Leave herbaceous and hollow-stemmed plants unpruned until early spring as they can provide homes for over-wintering insects.
- During mild spells of winter, hedgehogs can emerge from hibernation for a quick food foray before returning to their hiding places as the temperature drops. They will appreciate having some food left out for them. Hedgehog food is now available for sale or an alternative is canned dog food. Bread and milk are not suitable.

JOBS FOR THE MONTH

- All bird feeds are now safe so continue to put food out regularly.
- Keep the bird bath topped up and clean regularly (see Week 1).
- Make a hedgehog hibernation box.
- Leave seed heads standing to provide food and shelter for wildlife.
- Leave mature ivy uncut to flower. The nectar is a food source for insects.
- Make a leaf pile for hibernating mammals and overwintering ground-feeding birds.
- Empty and clean out nesting boxes with boiling water. When thoroughly dry, place a handful of wood shavings inside. It may provide winter shelter. It is illegal to remove unhatched eggs except between November and January.
- Regularly shake off leaves from nets over ponds. Rake out leaves from ponds that are not netted.

NOVEMBER

First quarter   *Monday* 4

Guy Fawkes   *Tuesday* 5

Wednesday 6

Thursday 7

Friday 8

Saturday 9

Remembrance Sunday   *Sunday* 10

NOVEMBER

11 *Monday*

12 *Tuesday*

Full moon

13 *Wednesday*

14 *Thursday*

15 *Friday*

16 *Saturday*

17 *Sunday*

Long-tailed tits (*Aegithalos caudatus*)

NOVEMBER

Monday 18

Last quarter

Tuesday 19

Wednesday 20

Thursday 21

Friday 22

Saturday 23

Sunday 24

Dunnock (*Prunella modularis*)

NOVEMBER & DECEMBER

25 *Monday*

26 *Tuesday*   *New moon*

27 *Wednesday*

28 *Thursday*   Holiday, USA (Thanksgiving Day)

29 *Friday*

30 *Saturday*   St. Andrew's Day

1 *Sunday*   First Sunday in Advent

Barn owl (*Tyto alba*)

'Plant berry-producing shrubs and trees to provide a winter food source for birds. They bring colour to the garden too!'

JOBS FOR THE MONTH

- Top up bird feeders and put food out on the ground and bird tables. Once a feeding regime is established try and keep to it as this will encourage birds to return.
- All bird feed, including peanuts, are safe as the breeding season is over (see Week 18).
- Keep the bird bath topped up and ice free.
- Clean birdbaths and tables regularly.
- Where possible leave seed heads standing to provide food and shelter for wildlife.
- If possible leave mature ivy uncut to flower.
- Make a leaf pile for hibernating mammals and over-wintering ground-feeding birds.

INSECTS

Butterflies and moths hibernate through the winter in places that are sheltered from wind, frost and rain. They prefer a habitat of evergreen plants and thick tangles of leaves and stems so either plant shrubs to encourage them or give yourself a break from pruning.

PLANT FOR WILDLIFE

- Planting a single tree provides a host of habitats for a wide variety of insects and mammals. Native trees will always support more wildlife than imported varieties.
- Consider planting more shrubs and trees that produce berries in order to provide a valuable food source for garden birds. Red and orange berries are reported to be more popular with birds than yellow berries.
- Holly (*Ilex*) is a traditional part of Christmas; however, holly berries are a valuable source of food for birds, so don't take them all for Christmas! In spring Holly Blue butterfly larvae feed on holly flower buds and berries.
- Native ivy is also very good for wildlife. The flowers feed bees, butterflies and hoverflies, and the thick tangle of stems and leaves make winter homes for many butterflies and other insects. The birds eat the berries too.

DECEMBER

Monday 2

Tuesday 3

First quarter

Wednesday 4

Thursday 5

Friday 6

Saturday 7

Sunday 8

DECEMBER

9 *Monday*

10 *Tuesday*

11 *Wednesday*

12 *Thursday*   *Full moon*

13 *Friday*

14 *Saturday*

15 *Sunday*

Song thrush (*Turdus philomelos*)

DECEMBER

Monday 16

Tuesday 17

Wednesday 18

Last quarter

Thursday 19

Friday 20

Winter Solstice (Winter begins)

Saturday 21

Winter Solstice (Winter begins
Hanukkah begins (at sunset)

Sunday 22

Robin (*Erithacus rubecula*)

DECEMBER

---

23 *Monday*

---

24 *Tuesday*   Christmas Eve

---

25 *Wednesday*

Christmas Day
Holiday, UK, Republic of Ireland, USA, Canada,
Australia and New Zealand

---

26 *Thursday*

New moon
Boxing Day (St. Stephen's Day)
Holiday, UK, Republic of Ireland, Canada,
Australia and New Zealand

---

27 *Friday*

---

28 *Saturday*

---

29 *Sunday*

Blue tit (*Parus caeruleus*)

DECEMBER & JANUARY 2020

Hanukkah ends

Monday 30

New Year's Eve

Tuesday 31

New Year's Day
Holiday, UK, Republic of Ireland, USA, Canada,
Australia and New Zealand

Wednesday 1

Holiday, Scotland and New Zealand

Thursday 2

Friday 3

Saturday 4

Sunday 5

Blackbird (*Turdus merula*)

YEAR PLANNER

JANUARY	JULY
FEBRUARY	AUGUST
MARCH	SEPTEMBER
APRIL	OCTOBER
MAY	NOVEMBER
JUNE	DECEMBER